BELIEVE IN YOUYOURSELF

Kendra,
God Bless,
May God fulfill your
Dreams

© 2014, James Sutton Jr., Mount Holly, NC

ALL RIGHTS RESERVED. No part of this book may be reproduced or transmitted in any form or by any means without written permission from the author.

To God be the Glory

I give all honor to God who strengthens me and provides me with knowledge and direction. I thank you Lord for allowing me to reach others in a way which is unique and informative. Thank you for giving me the gifts, talents, and the ability to lead others and get results. All I do and all I will ever do is magnify You.

At His Feet

In Loving Memory of

James H. Sutton Sr.

Mommy

You are an amazing woman. The strength and love we witnessed as you cared for your husband, our father, was remarkable. We are truly blessed to have you as our Mom. While Dad is not with us in the flesh, please take comfort in knowing, you both instilled so much love into your children, Dad is ever present in us.

We love you Mommy,

Kim, Sabrina, Bill, Louie, Todd, Malik

Jeannett

I thank my beautiful wife Jeannett for listening and helping me talk myself through my antics. I learned so much about being myself because of you. You have allowed me to vent and helped me stay focused on God's plan for me & for us. Most importantly, you taught me the power of prayer.

He who finds a wife finds what is good
and receives favor from the LORD.
(NIV, Proverbs 18:22)

A Message to My Children

I know you will face some challenges in life. I want you both to continue to do your best. My only hope for you is to continue to put God first. Allow God to illuminate your gifts and talents and always use them for His glory. You must believe in yourself and know you can accomplish anything you set your heart and mind to do.

> Love Mommy
>
> Jeannett Sutton

Acknowledgements

I thank God for my children and grandchildren – doing better is the optimum word:

Lemar, Janelle, Sasha, Malcolm, Jenae

My Children outside the Blood - Tysean, Shernette, Shari, Kristin

Thank You God for our parents:

James & Theresa
John & Patricia

My brothers and sisters, you are all remarkable and you have all planted a seed in me to make me who I am today: Thank You!

Kim, Sabrina, Louis, Todd, Malik
Donna, Tondia, Precola, John Jr.

A special thank you to my Coney Island Cathedral, CORE, and New Hope International Church Families – in particular the members of our Life Group; it's amazing how God lined everything up for us to this point.

Special Thanks to Baron Samuel Author of "Best Days Worst Nights" & "The Gentlemen's Club" for the cover art inspiration and design.

About the Author

James Sutton Jr. is the Campus President at Virginia College in Macon, GA. James has over 30 years' experience in Recruitment, Management and Personal Development. He has conducted dozens of workshops to motivate and encourage others to succeed. His books "Look at Your Boss! Rehabilitation for Your Career," and "Effective Leaders: Mentor People and Manage Processes were well received by his target audience of young adults to inspire them to finish school, get training, and not settle for their current place in life.

James is a 23 year retired United States Air Force and United States Marine Corp Veteran. He is the recipient of 'The Airman's Medal' for Heroism.

James is a licensed Minister under the tutelage of Bishop Waylyn Hobbs Jr., Senior Pastor of Coney Island Cathedral of Deliverance in Brooklyn, NY.

He has served as an Elder at CORE Church, Mount Holly, NC - Pastor Tim McCarn is Senior Pastor.

And Servant Leader with New Hope Bible Institute in Fort Valley, GA – Pastor Jordan Poole is Senior Pastor

Take a moment to find your three

You are Beautiful Quotes:

_____

_____

_____

Me

_____

_____

_____

Me

_____

_____

_____

Me

STOP!!! GO BACK A PAGE!!!

Go back and fill in the blank lines for quotes about your beauty. Not just your physical beauty, but your inward beauty.

Forward

Romans 12:6-7

Having gifts that differ according to the grace given to us, let us use them: if prophecy, in proportion to our faith; if service, in our serving; the one who teaches, in his teaching

The conversation begins...

Sometimes we find ourselves paying more attention to someone else's life instead of refining, defining, and living our own life. I want you to take some time to examine your life. I want you to look at yourself through the lens of your own eyes and forget about everyone else. Don't look at your reflection and imagine who you can be like... look at your reflection and ask yourself... 'Who am I'?

When you look at your life whether you're young or not so young, try to rehash the blue print and the direction you have travelled – have you veered off course? Are you your worst enemy – or should I say "inner me?"

> Once you defeat your "inner me" –
> You can then "Be You"

Table of Contents

Chapter 1: Work of Wonder

Chapter 2: Where is Your Heart?

Chapter 3: Mind Blowing

Chapter 4: Materialistic Dreams

Chapter 5: Future Plans

Chapter 6: Supernatural

Chapter 7: You're Not Alone

Chapter 8: It's Your Time

Chapter 9: Walk the Talk

Chapter 1

Work of Wonder

Psalm 139:14-16 ESV

Praise you, for I am fearfully and wonderfully made. Wonderful are your works; my soul knows it very well. My frame was not hidden from you, when I was being made in secret, intricately woven in the depths of the earth. Your eyes saw my unformed substance; in your book were written, every one of them, the days that were formed for me, when as yet there was none of them.

> *I spent many years of my life trying to figure out my purpose. Most of the time it ended with me thinking and talking about the things I wasn't capable of achieving. The self-doubt crept in and then the only thing I would focus on was the time lost. This led to me shrugging my shoulders and saying "oh well, this is my life." ~ Jamesism*

Develop a Positive Vision of Yourself

Close your eyes for five seconds… then open them so you can finish reading the book. Now go to the mirror – (take a moment to find a mirror because it is critical to this exercise). Now close your eyes for five seconds then open them.

What does your physical reflection present that your mental reflection is lacking? I am not talking about your height and weight or the pimple on your nose. I am talking about your inner person. When you close your eyes and think about yourself, are you Spiderman or Batman? Who are you when you close your eyes? Now, what happens when you open them?

> What does your physical reflection present that your mental reflection is lacking?

Think of a time when you didn't have a belief in yourself and it held you back. Now think of someone you admire – Close your eyes and think about how they would handle the situation.

What did you see someone else accomplish you couldn't accomplish yourself?

Self-Limitations

When you were born, you had no limitations. You had no idea what you could or couldn't achieve. You had no limits and you had over the top expectations. You had a superhero mentality. I remember running around the house with my brother and sisters and from all accounts we were superheroes. As I recall... I was Spiderman, my brother Louie was Superman (he used a towel as a cape), and I forget whether it was my sister Kim or Sabrina who was Wonder Woman. We had no limits... no limitations.

There was a point in your life when you dreamed of things you wanted to accomplish and there was no stopping you.

> Once you defeat your "inner me" –You can then "Be You"

Sometimes, I sit here wondering and asking myself, when did I learn limitations? When did it become easier to believe "I can't"? What happened to the belief of "I can" and "I will?" – Do you remember saying ~ "I dare you or anyone else to try and stop me from achieving my dreams." – What happened to your boldness? When did you stop believing in the plan God laid out for you? Did you ever know the plan? When did you start down this path of deception? And finally, who put your fire out?

In order to move forward, you have to unlearn the limits you placed on your ability to accomplish the perceived impossible. You must ask yourself what it will take for you to regain your superhero mentality. If God laid out the plan, regardless of the path you took...

As long as we resubmit to His instructions, we are directed back on course... Right?

Isn't it funny now that you are thinking about it?

It's funny because what you believe about yourself is who you have become; ironically, isn't true. All this time you have been wrapped up in your own deception about yourself. All this time, the doubt and inability to accomplish your dreams was limited from your own thoughts and beliefs about yourself.

The tricky part about knowing the plan created for you... is realizing there was a plan and there is still a plan in existence. Somehow we talked ourselves into working and believing our own plan. You put "THE PLAN" on the back burner.

Is there something you do every day which brings you joy? Is there something you do for someone else that brings you joy? I've found as we dig deeper into the plan we have for ourselves; the plan for happiness, always encompasses improving and pouring into the lives of others. I've found through the numerous counseling sessions I conducted, the plan is rarely about self-fulfillment or self-gratification. It's almost always about what we do for others. But it starts with a belief in self.

Self-Belief

It's time for your introduction. Yes, I want you to meet "You" for the very first time. To believe in yourself, you have to meet "You" where you stand then get to know "You". If you met yourself for the first time, what would be your first impression? Now – stop – when you thought about yourself whose voice did you hear?

Remember, this is not about what other people say or think about you. It's time to find yourself and convince yourself that you are not all the negative things you believe yourself to be.

> In order to 'Be You" take a minute to get to know you.

So let's start by introducing "You" to you. Self-belief starts with tapping into the positive characteristics which make up your 'YOU'; that make up who you are. Are you so beaten down you cannot find one nice thing to say about you?

Who is the person that co- signs on all your misery? I want you to listen to that voice (just for a minute). They said something nice about you at least once.

I am talking about the soothing ear person that is going to nod at everything you say; or the mental co-signer looking for a partner in misery.

If you don't have anyone to call, let's make a list of characteristics you feel you possess.

Remember, this is about mental development. In the HR world, we talk about having a "30 second elevator speech" to describe yourself to a potential employer. Go ahead and do it. If you're in a public place reading this book, talk into your phone, we don't want folk thinking you're crazy.

Ready, set... go!

How hard was that? Were you able to positively talk about yourself for 30 seconds? Start thinking about some positive characteristics you expect to see in others. Do you see them in YOUrself... no really!
Ask yourself the hard questions. – look at yourself to see if you have any of those characteristics. Think positive; with positive being the optimum word.
You are renewing your mind... Here are some characteristics to consider:

I find it easy to talk to people
I have a positive attitude
I handle pressure situations
I have a sense of humor
I take constructive criticism
I give my time and talents
I think quickly on my feet
I am educated (from books or the street)
I am charismatic
I am popular

Yea, there are a lot of 'I's" in there. It's your list. As you're creating your list, really think about what each statement means to you and how effectively you execute each aspect of the sentence you read. Are you being realistic?

Next, take the list and jot down what you need to improve on in each of the characteristics you laid out.

For instance:

I handle situations well (after I calm down). That means you have to work on not blowing up.

I give my time and talents (but their meetings are too long and I don't like the leaders). You have to learn to work on other people's terms.

You are filled with many positive characteristics that have been suppressed or have gone unnoticed by you. So, how do you like you so far?

Self-Encouragement

1 Samuel 30:6 (ESV) And David was greatly distressed, for the people spoke of stoning him, because all the people were bitter in soul, each for his sons and daughters. But David strengthened himself in the Lord his God.

Once you make up your mind to make positive deposits into YOUrself – you can be transformed into your positive view of YOUrself- ~ then you will need fewer deposits from peanut gallery to validate who you are. Ok... here is the tricky part.

In some aspects of religion and church, we depend on the pastors to be the motivational speaker in our lives and not just provide the spiritual guidance. The Praise and Worship team provides the theme music and not assist in setting the atmosphere. And the rest of the congregation becomes the judge and jury.

We all need a relevant Word from God.

When the naysayers came against David, he didn't wait until Sunday or Wednesday to be refueled; he encouraged and strengthened himself. Sometimes we have to be our own cheerleader.

Rah, Rah Me!

When you start your day with your theme music (we will discuss later in this chapter), rehearse your elevator speech, and then remember all the things you are capable of doing. You will begin doing mental backflips and landing with a 10!

Inner Voice

If you read my last book *Effective Leaders: Mentor People and Manage Processes* – you see the discussion I have with my inner voice. My inner voice is inquisitive, encouraging, and straight to the point. My inner voice and I have a "love-love" relationship. It didn't always work that way. I use to hate the things I would say to myself; about myself. It took many soul searching journeys to take control of my inner voice. What type of verbal exchange do you have with your inner voice? Is that voice an ally or an enemy? By who, what, and when was your voice developed? Who shaped that voice? Whose voice do you hear in your mind when decisions are being made about your life?

Understand the voices you hear will come from various sources based on the experiences you had throughout your life. I've heard my grandma's voice, my Nanny, Papa Nick, my Mother, Father, sister and brothers, friends, enemies, pastors, teachers, and even strangers; I've heard voices from movies and sitcoms. Heck, I ain't ashamed to say I even heard bugs bunny and numerous cartoon characters from my childhood. These are the voices that shape your decisions and often time promote or limit your actions. These voices attempt to define you. However, if bugs bunny gives me advice, I have to think twice about the source… I must realize Bugs Bunny isn't always right ~ just saying

How often do you hear God's Voice; the voice from the knowledge of His Word? I aint getting preachy on you ~ But He said you are "fearfully and wonderfully made~ Wonderful are your works; my soul knows it very well."

Fearful Spirit

Have you ever done something out of fear or with a fearful spirit? You may think that means scared – But fearfully in this context is out of perfection! No mistakes, no excuses! You have been created with precision – it's time to release the thoughts that minimize who you are. ~ "Silly Rabbit, tricks are for Kids"~ When did these voices start to turn on you?

When you hear your inner voice, the first thing you need to do is look at the source. Is it in alignment and in direction of God's Word? If not, why are you giving that voice so much power over your actions? Where did the source get its power over you?

If my broke friend is giving me advice on finances…; I must disregard the advice on money management but listen to how he mismanaged. If my single friend is giving me advice on my marriage, I may need to disregard some of the advice on making my marriage last but I may need to listen to the things that destroyed his marriage. If a dreamer is giving me advice on my vision… disregard!

Segmentation

Who and what makes up your inner voice? It's time for you to separate the voices that lead to your decisions and the perception you have of yourself! Focus on Y. O. U. not I.O.U. – You owe no one anything but you owe yourself everything.

Putting your inner voice into the proper segment is critical for improving how you feel about you. As I engage individuals in search of themselves, I have found most of them are battling with what others have said about them as opposed to what is in front of them; consider the source. Yes, you will hear consider the source over and over from me in this book; so, consider the source.

> You owe no one anything but you owe yourself everything. ~ Jamesism

When the disciples told Jesus that folk was telling them various things about him - the only thing Jesus said was "who do you say I am?" ~Matthew 16:13~ (NIV)

As you consider the various sources which have forged your thinking about YOUrself ~ how much weight do you give those thoughts? Are the thoughts negative or positive?

At My Worst

Have you heard this saying, "I am my worst critic" ~ "I am hard on myself" ~ Have you ever said this to yourself? Why are you so hard on yourself? What actions have you taken to improve upon the critiques?

> Sometimes we have to be our own cheerleader.

I didn't start believing in myself until I became my greatest cheerleader!

Once I realized the voices in my head weren't in the tone of my voice ~ I started the process of change. When I didn't just hear bugs bunny, nana, and them, and I started hearing my own voice; I started to change!

> I didn't start believing in myself until I became my greatest cheerleader!

When you start criticizing yourself – what voice do you hear? Instead of saying I am my worst critic – become your greatest ally. Become the "can do" voice not the "won't do" voice. Leave the 'Debbie Downer's' of your life at the curb. Most importantly, don't be a Downer to YOUrself. Find your inner voice; listen to your inner voice. Stop listening to respond and listen to comprehend. We have to deal with the inner me so you are able to face the outer me.

Attitude Adjustment

Romans 12: (NIV)

2 Do not conform to the pattern of this world, but be transformed by the renewing of your mind.

One of my favorite sayings is "doing a check-up from the neck up." To adjust your attitude, we have to adjust our mind. Bishop Waylyn Hobbs Jr.'s Book "New Mind, New You" nails this biblical concept.

You have been created without a flaw; but know you are not perfect. The mind must be renewed and reconditioned to find your true self.

How do you recondition your mind after years and years of battering? After years and years of believing your self-worth aint what it ought to be? The simple answer...

Theme Music

Before every speech or presentation I give, I like to start with my theme song "Gonna Fly Now" the theme from the movie 'Rocky'. It's something about hearing the horns in the beginning of the song that gets the fire burning inside of me. Did you hear it in your mind – did you see the pictures of a man punching on beef and running up steps in

Philadelphia come to my mind. Never staying down on the canvas, just getting back up! Overcoming!

What song do you play when you have stuff on your mind? When the voices are going off in your head condemning and torturing you? What songs are you listening to?

Saints... some of those songs you listen too about the testimony... well (in my church voice), if you focus on the testimony and not the overcoming. You are wallowing in the problem and not hearing the solution. Do you like the song because of the beginning and are you getting to the end? It's inspirational but you focus on the going through and not the fight through.

> It's inspirational but you focus on the going through and not the fight through.

What is your theme song? The how you lost your love song... or the I am so alone song, don't count! What is your theme song? Is it triumphant?

Your theme song needs to focus on what is right about you. You have to walk away from that song with a self-belief and determination that will push you to want to improve who you are. Have you ever listened to a song that makes you want to run out the door and tackle the world?

Motivational Music

Listen to any motivational speaker and I am talking about some preachers. They walk up to the podium after a good motivational and inspirational rendition of something; then blow you away.

I know I should call this book the book of questions. You see, it's the unanswered or unasked questions that have you doubting yourself. The beautiful thing is all the questions will be at the back of the book. If you can answer them, you have transformed who you are. In order to 'Be You" take a minute to get to know you. As a matter of fact have you ever met you? The real you... keep it 100! you? The real you... keep it 100!

Deck the "Halls"

The next time you are in the store, pick up a bag of "Halls" cough drops. Each drop is wrapped in a "pep talk." If you don't have a cold save the drop and read the wrapper.

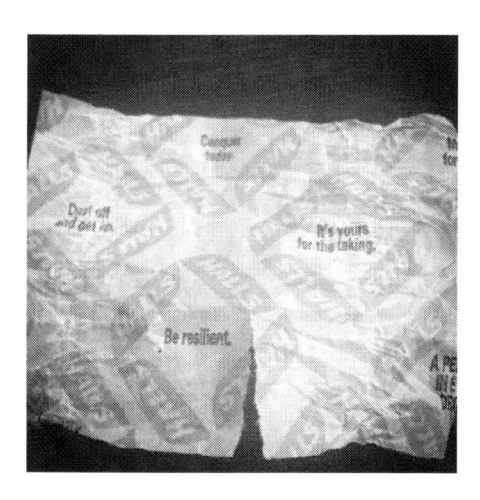

Re-Cap

Psalm 139:14-16 ESV ~ Praise you, for I am fearfully and wonderfully made. Wonderful are your works; my soul knows it very well.

1. **Vision of Yourself**
2. **Self-Limitations**
3. **Self-Belief**
4. **Self-Encouragement**
5. **Inner Voice**
6. **Segmentation of the Inner Voice**
7. **Attitude Adjustment**
8. **Theme Music**

Embracing the fact you are made to perfection and to perform within perfection is not a sign of arrogance. You need to be confident in your Creator and have the confidence in yourself. It's only the first step to believing in you.

Get into the habit of sitting down, closing your eyes, and watching yourself behave decisively, calmly, and with strength. This powerful visualization exercise means you can learn from yourself how to be confident, have self-belief, and behave in ways you use to imagine.

Take a minute to answer a few questions and then discuss them with your group:

How do you view yourself among your peers?

1. _____
2. _____
3. _____

What are your three greatest attributes?

1. _____
2. _____
3. _____

How do you encourage yourself?

1. _____
2. _____
3. _____

What limits have you placed on your life?

1. _____
2. _____
3. _____

Whose voice do you hear when you make decisions?

1. _____

2. _____

3. _____

Do you read the Bible?

1. _____

2. _____

3. _____

How often do you pray?

1. _____

2. _____

3. _____

What is your motivational theme song?

1. _____

2. _____

3. _____

Chapter 2

Where is Your Heart?

1 Samuel 16:7 ESV

But the Lord said to Samuel, "Do not look on his appearance or on the height of his stature, because I have rejected him. For the Lord sees not as man sees: man looks on the outward appearance, but the Lord looks on the heart."

Inner Me 2.0 – Self Limitations

We have established a few things in the first chapter. First, you HAVE the goods as a matter of fact, you are the Goods! Your thinking is changing – if not you need to start this book over. Go back and redefine your characteristics. Sit down with someone you trust who is non-judgmental but is willing to tell you the truth.

Sometimes I speak to people that want to hear the truth but don't want me to tell them the truth. They continue to get caught up in the same situation and wonder why. If you are like most people, there is a long list of people that will tell you what is wrong with you. Some do it to keep you down; others do it to lift you out of a bad place. A good pulse test to see which side they are on is their relevance to the scripture. This is the time to check the "I's" - If they keep saying "I think…" hmmm ~Overtime with the right people around you, you will start to feel the refueling from your daily thoughts.

Somewhere, you lost the "I can do anything" mentality, which created fear – You were no longer fearless. As you marinate in the "I can," Let's take a harder look at the enemy that has plagued your thinking. Let's look at the inner-me portion from a different perspective. Did you see how you read over the words "enemy" and "inner me" as if it were the same word?

Is it me or is there a lot of talk today about a person's appearance? How you look on the outside?

Facebook has an obsession with selfies – they are not all bad but do the outer me live up to the inner me. I see a lot of people living double lives on social media. There is a lot of good that can come from social media as well.

If you're a fan of social media then you may have seen the YouTube Video posted by T.D. Jakes "Junk in Your Trunk"- look it up!

The video on YouTube showed the outside of cars; beautiful and expensive cars. When he opened the trunk; the trunks were full of stuff… junk…. thing-a-ma-gigs. If we opened you up today, what will the contents reveal? Who are you? When you were putting together that 30 second "me" speech, how much was fluff? How much were you trying to be the person who you wanted to be as opposed to the person that you are?

Societal Vanity

We have a vain society. You will find many of us are not like God in the sense we treat people a certain way based on their appearance.

> You need to stop trying to impress other people.

I remember visiting an economics business class and the instructor said "In the service industry or hotel industry they treat people on the higher floors different then the folk on the lower floors." How do you treat people?

Do you have the correct outward appearance? That was a trick question. As you discover who you are, your outward appearance will begin to reflect who you are on the inside. A great deal of yourself will be a reflection what is on your heart.

As you continue through the discovery process of self, you will undoubtedly find things that make you feel good and things which make you feel uncomfortable.

You need to stop trying to impress other people.

Let us pray!

Take a minute to answer a few questions and then discuss them with your group:

Do you rate people based on what they are wearing?

1. _____

2. _____

3. _____

Do you spend more time in the mirror or the Word?

1. _____

2. _____

3. _____

How many selfies do you take and post a day?

1. _____

2. _____

3. _____

Do you treat all people the same?

1. _____

2. _____

3. _____

What did you think about T.D. Jakes video "junk"?

1. _____
2. _____
3. _____

Does your outward appearance reflect who you are?

1. _____
2. _____
3. _____

How often do you pray?

1. _____
2. _____
3. _____

Do you live to impress people?

1. _____
2. _____
3. _____

Chapter 3

Mind Blowing

Romans 12:2 ESV

Do not be conformed to this world, but be transformed by the renewal of your mind, that by testing you may discern what is the will of God, what is good and acceptable and perfect.

> *"James, now you know what they say about assumptions..."*
> *says the inner voice*

Mental Assessment

There is a test. Like most things in the religious realm we tend to stop short when discerning the scriptures largely because we don't read the whole verse. I am sure as you read Romans 12:2 you knew:

> "Do not be conformed to this world, but be transformed by the renewal of the mind,"

But there is no period after mind. There is a comma after "renewal of the mind" – this implies/means there is more. So the reality is you only knew and understood Romans 12 and a half. To understand Romans 12:2 you MUST continue reading. As we continue reading, we find there is a test. And the beautiful thing is we initiate the test.

"...that by testing you may discern what is the will of God,"

What does this mean in relationship to you "being you?" There are many things you will try and there are many things you will succeed in doing. That does not mean they are in line with the will of God. You have to test and discern God's will. As your mind is continuously renewed and you start to find your purpose, the test will be the ultimate indicator of the place you need to be in your life.

> So the reality is you only knew and understood Romans 12 and a half.

But there is no period there. There is a comma; after renewal of the mind—there is more.

"...what is good and acceptable and perfect."

This is where the perfection is displayed. When you begin to find your purpose. Now comes the period in the verse. Simply put, do not conform and be transformed. We discern through testing, what is good and acceptable and perfect. Notice the "and" between the results! Each is required!

The Plan

Step back and take a look at yourself. Then take a look at the world. Remember, you are a part of the world but you don't have to conform to the world's standard.

There are three basic needs in life: love, purpose, and significance. The most important thing to remember is one cannot find significance in their job or the work they do. In Ecclesiastes 2:4-11, Solomon explains how he looked for meaning in various activities from being an owner to a hard worker. While his work was fulfilling, he surmise in verse eleven:

> There are three basic needs in life: love, purpose and significance.

"Yet when I surveyed all that my hands had done and what I had toiled to achieve, everything was meaningless, a chasing after the wind; nothing was gained under the sun."

How much time do you spend chasing a dream that is not purposed? How much time do you spend searching the scriptures, praying, and discerning the moves you make based on the test? Is it good and acceptable and perfect in the eyes of God?

Inner Voice 2.0

As your mind is renewed the verbal exchange with your inner voice will begin to change. When we stop trying to conform to the standards of people and the things they put in front of us, we are able to discern the things we were called to do in our lives.

Through the years the problems you faced were less about you and more about what you thought people wanted you to do. Everyone has a plan for your life. Grant it there have been people in your life that have been placed there to give you guidance. You must define if they are your enemy or your ally.

Please remember your ally is not going to allow you to do the things they know will hurt you.

> We move forward without discernment – without a test – and without measuring it against Good, Acceptable, and Perfect (GAP)!

The voice I want you to pay attention to is the voice inside of you. Most of the time we know something is wrong but we continue working in it and hope it will change. Sometimes we operate with unrealistic expectations. We move forward without discernment – without a test – and without measuring it against Good, Acceptable, and Perfect (GAP) standards! When you hear someone say they are standing in the GAP for you, discern if their stand passes the litmus test of Good, Acceptable and Perfect.

Look No Further

Ezekiel 22:23-30 30 "I looked for a man among them who would build up the wall and stand before me in the gap on behalf of the land so I would not have to destroy it, but I found none.

We don't always find someone to stand in the GAP on our behalf ~ we spend a lot of time creating the wall between what we need to achieve and what we want to achieve- and most importantly what we actually achieve. ~Jamesism

Standing in the GAP

Definition of "the gap" = that space between what is and what God says ought to be.

> We spend a lot of time creating the wall between what we need to achieve and what we want to achieve

As we choose our words we need to know there is a time for everything but it is hard to self-heal when we are the authors of the GAP in our lives. When we allow our past to control the things in our future; we stifle our inner voice and make it obsolete.

Some gaps never self-heal! Time never makes them better, go away, or disappear. God sees this gap in Ezekiel 22:23-30, and was looking for somebody to stand in it. But no one was there!

The renewing of our minds fills the GAPS – but the test results must reveal what is Good, Acceptable, and Perfect!

Paul shared 2 Timothy 3:16- 17 "All scripture is given by inspiration of God, and is profitable for doctrine, for reproof, for correction, for instruction in righteousness: That the man of God may be complete, thoroughly furnished unto all good works."

Final Transformation

As part of our transformation we are to "prove" the good, acceptable, complete will of God, then that will also make us complete. Paul shared it is all in the scriptures.

Simply put, the perfect will of God is found by studying the entire Bible. There is no one scripture that states it, but the totality of scripture is the key.

The inner voice, your inner voice needs to be the voice of God – God's voice is found in the scriptures.

Take a minute to answer a few questions and then discuss them with your group:

How do you work on the three basic needs (p. 28)?

1. _____
2. _____
3. _____

Do you understand the GAP concept?

1. _____
2. _____
3. _____

Do you discern before you make a decision?

1. _____
2. _____
3. _____

What actions do you take to renew your mind?

1. _____
2. _____
3. _____

Can God use you to stand in the GAP for others?

1. _____

2. _____

3. _____

What do you use as a basic to correct your behavior?

1. _____

2. _____

3. _____

How often do you pray?

1. _____

2. _____

3. _____

Whose voice is your inner voice?

1. _____

2. _____

3. _____

Chapter 4

Materialistic Dreams

1 Peter 3:3-4 ESV

Do not let your adorning be external—the braiding of hair and the putting on of gold jewelry, or the clothing you wear— but let your adorning be the hidden person of the heart with the imperishable beauty of a gentle and quiet spirit, which in God's sight is very precious.

I'm Going In

Whew... where do I begin? There is a come as you are mentality in the world that has curtailed the "wake up and be somebody" mindset of the nineties. I wish it were just in the world; but it's in the Church – Somebody shout "Church" - Is Church being transformed with the world. Because it's one thing to come as you are, it's another to come as you aint got time to put it all together. There used to be a place that taught and exemplified family. Stop!!! – don't condemn me I was making a point! People it doesn't matter – James 2:1 (EVS) shared *"My brothers, show no partiality as you hold the faith in our Lord Jesus Christ, the Lord of glory."*

The Dash

Let me get back on the topic. Look at the first verse in 1 Peter 3:3 ~ "Do not let your adorning be external" DASH!

Becoming you is internal. This takes us back to Chapter 2 – it's about the heart!

I know you want the new Jordan's, the MK purses, the bling and the blang! There is nothing wrong with being blessed and living a wonderful life... unless... your adorning represents a false picture of who you are and who you have been called to be.

You have to beautify the inner you before you can beautify the outer you. Did you get a chance to look at T.D. Jakes video about the "Junk in the Trunk" – When you start to cleanse the mind and unveil the needs of the heart – (basically you need a blood transfusion) you will be able to separate the wants and the needs.

You will be able to wear the Jordan's knowing you stayed true to that which was in you. I had a discussion with my team today and we talked about going after the things you want.

Financial Adjustment (sidebar)

When we talked about finances one of my team members implied he didn't make enough money to do the things he wanted to do. After he finished, I shared he made more than enough money and to monitor if he was living outside of your means.

If you are working and your outcome surpasses your income the only adjustment to be made is with your spending. This is where preparation comes in. This is where planning comes in. This is where you ask do you need to make a change… Oops that was in my first book – Look at Your Boss ~Rehabilitation for Your Career, PICK IT up!

Vision of Yourself

> When you spend most of your time presenting false airs about yourself you become that person externally but you are dying inside.

When you spend most of your time presenting false airs about yourself you become that person externally but you are dying inside. I meet people all the time that try to present themselves more by doing more name dropping then living. They spend a lot of time talking about the accomplishments of others around them and they forget the things they accomplished themselves.

For example, when I assist people in writing their resumes, I ask them to make a list of things that they have done in the scope of their jobs. Often time they come back with a short list which does not tell the whole story of what they do. Who are you and what are the hopes and dreams you want to achieve. When you look in the mirror at your adorning, can you honestly say that is who you are?

Now I want you to look nice. I am a propionate of dressing for success. My grandmother Nanny never left the house unless she was "cleaner than the board of health. I remember taking her to the grocery store to get a head of lettuce (she had to pick the lettuce herself), it took her longer to get dressed than it took to go to the store, pick the lettuce, and drive back.

The picture I am talking about is the one that pains you every day. That picture in your mind of you all dressed up for the ball but like Cinderella, you are waiting for it all to disappear. You're dressed up on the outside but you are tore apart on the inside.

You dressed yourself from the outside in. I want to encourage you to look in the mirror and dress yourself from the inside out.

What is on your mind? What barriers do you see when you talk to yourself about where you need to be.

When you begin to see that your adorning is not based on the designer wear you crave, you will find yourself with more designer wear... that thing called favor and blessings.

Take a minute to answer a few questions and then discuss them with your group:

Does your designer wear dictate your personality?

1. _____
2. _____
3. _____

How do you act on bad hair days?

1. _____
2. _____
3. _____

How much do you embellish minor details?

1. _____
2. _____
3. _____

Do you take pride in your appearance?

1. _____
2. _____
3. _____

Which is most important the internal/external you?

1. _____

2. _____

3. _____

Do you present false airs to impress people?

1. _____

2. _____

3. _____

How often do you pray?

1. _____

2. _____

3. _____

Are you ready for Favor and Blessings?

1. _____

2. _____

3. _____

Chapter 5

Future Plans

1 Peter 3:3-4 ESV

For I know the plans I have for you, declares the Lord, plans for welfare and not for evil, to give you a future and a hope.

Moving Forward

By now you should have given some thought about how you see yourself and what is the measuring stick you use to define who you are.

> You're fearfully and wonderfully made

> You have a Good heart

> You know you must measure in the GAP

> Your adorning is internal

How then do you take what has been presented and apply it to your life?

You already started if you made it this far in this book. You should already look at yourself differently. Things are starting to click and you can understand that it's a façade to continue to pretend to be someone you're not. You will never find out who you are if you continue to live in the shadow of someone else.

Anytime I have a discussion with someone about their future I question their commitment. I received an email yesterday from someone I spoke to two years ago. He stated he took my advice and has started to change his life. He said it took two years but he is applying it now.

Will it take another two years for you to make the necessary changes to be comfortable in your own skin? Do you have more excuses than you have results? The excuse chapter in this book will be shorter than the one in Look at Your Boss. The chapter on excuses in Look at Your Boss was one page. You just finished the one sentence on excuses in this book.

How do we get it done? Remember all the answers lie within the scriptures. I put the questions in the final chapter. If you don't attend a church that offers Bible Study – Find a church or a group that study. I don't care what charade your church calls it but you can't get all you need from the pulpit. You MUST study the Word for yourself.

Team Me

Where is your commitment to self? You spend time encouraging her, you spend time encouraging him. I need you to join "Team Me" – If you want to be a cheerleader for a team, start with your own team.

When we moved to Georgia last year – I uprooted my family from Charlotte, N.C; I broke a promise to my wife and kids. When I retired from the Air Force, I told them that was it, no more moving. We bought a house, settled down, and for 7 years we were good. Then that promotion opportunity came and we prayed on it… and here I am.

The major concerns we had were the fact that my daughter made the dance team at her former high school and her new school did not have a dance team. Everyone knows the challenge of high school girl and making the team and her daddy ruined it for her… need I say more. My son was in JROTC and moving away going into the 11th grade was going to limit his promotion and participation opportunities. Not!!!

A year later my son is Deputy Commander of his High School JROTC and my daughter is co-captain of the dance team she helped establish in her new high school.

Proverbs 16:3 - *Commit your work to the Lord, and your plans will be established.*

Simplicity

You have to be your own cheerleader. You have to commit yourself to a few things to get over self. The future plans to being you are simple:

Pray

Stop Embellishing

Stop Name Dropping

Commit

Take Action

Pray

Joshua 24:15 But as for me and my house, we will serve the LORD.

Sibling Rivalry (sidebar)

My brother, sisters and I have a sibling rivalry. We compete to give each other the most support. My younger brother Louis initiated prayer and brag calls. We pray for each other and talk about our blessings and needs. We learned to be genuinely happy for each other and this puts us in a position to help each other when we are in need of support. These calls have helped us in tough times and encourage us to be thankful today. If all families did this there would be a revival in every household.

Take a minute to answer a few questions and then discuss them with your group:

How often do you put yourself down?

1. _____
2. _____
3. _____

Do you feel you don't measure up to your peers?

1. _____
2. _____
3. _____

Write three nice things about yourself?

1. _____
2. _____
3. _____

Why is it so hard to cheer for yourself?

1. _____
2. _____
3. _____

How can you shake the victim mentality?

1. _____

2. _____

3. _____

Do you take pride in spreading gossip?

1. _____

2. _____

3. _____

Who are your role models?

1. _____

2. _____

3. _____

How often do you pray?

1. _____

2. _____

3. _____

Chapter 6

Supernatural

1 Corinthians 2:14 ESV

The natural person does not accept the things of the Spirit of God, for they are folly to him, and he is not able to understand them because they are spiritually discerned.

Stiffneck

Proverbs 29:11 NIV: A man who remains stiff-necked after many rebukes will suddenly be destroyed--without remedy.

I first researched the word Stiffneck when I graduated from Bible College and my wife's grandmother an Evangelist whom I respect and love, right before Prayer, she looked at me and stated "You're a Sniff-Neck" –then popped me on the back of the neck! It came out of the blue – I was not certain what she was talking about. So of course I questioned why she made the statement. I was not very familiar with the term and waited on her to explain. She did her grandma pause, looked me in the eye, and she said "You don't believe in nothing! - you have too much education and you don't rely on the Holy Spirit." I must have had an Arsenio Hall moment because I am sure my facial expression read "things that make you say hmmm." Through the years you learned not to argue with grandma; you especially don't question her on the bible. That night, I prayed and I diligently searched the scriptures, as I was taught in Bible College ☺. I wasn't certain if I was insulted or chastised; maybe both.

Acts 7:51 Ye stiffnecked and uncircumcised in heart and ears, ye do always resist the Holy Ghost: as your fathers did, so do ye.

The Bible is clear on the definition of sniff neck – One that resists the Holy Ghost. For the life of me I could not figure out why I was called out by my grandma about being one that did not rely on the Holy Spirit –

As you move forward I want you to start with Prayer. This seems to be lost form of expression in many churches. Some have even eliminated the prayer warriors that have been gifted to keep the walls erect and have the ability to stand in the GAP!

I understood the battle is not against flesh and blood. But here I am an Ox – The term stiff neck came from the fact that farmers used Oxen to plow fields in ancient Israel – The ox would stiffen its neck to prevent the farmer from going in the appropriate direction.

The Bible tells us to search the scriptures – Often time the congregation blindly listens to the Word being preached without doing their own due diligence of insuring the Word being preached is in line with the Word written. It requires one to search the scriptures.

Read the Bible! I echo time and again. Be a part of a group reading the scriptures and searching for clarification. It is not to say one does not believe what their pastor is saying but the Bereans were eager and examined daily what Paul spoke to insure it lined up with the Word of God.

> *Acts 17:11 NLT And the people of Berea were more open-minded than those in Thessalonica, and they listened eagerly to Paul's message. They searched the Scriptures day after day to see if Paul and Silas were teaching the truth.*

When we look at the parables and scriptures pertaining to Jesus ministry, the mindset of the ox plowing the land takes on deeper meaning. Jesus uses parables in relationship to the Harvest as a means to communicate to its followers.

We have embarked on a walk that has addressed some concerns – shed some light – and hopefully ended with accountability and discernment. This work is not meant to bash though some will receive its content as too direct. It is meant to be direct because we are in a time and at a place where we must hold each other accountable. Discerned.

My name is James – I was a Stiffneck – and Grandma should have popped me in the head twice. That pop in the head made me realize I needed to spend more time practicing the Word instead of just reading the Word.

Self-Belief

Self-confidence is good; it's not a bad thing. Lack of confidence is bad. Building your confidence is a process. It starts with a belief in you. It starts with you reaching back to your childhood mindset of believing in the Tooth Fairy... Santa Claus is real – the Easter Bunny is on the way. You need the Peter Pan mentality to a degree.

Believing you can conquer the world.

> It is sad but true that one's spiritual belief is often paralleled with one's personal belief.

I had a discussion with a young lady this morning and she looked up her name and it meant low esteemed, lack of confidence etc. and while she was reading all the negative stuff, I saw her co-signing on it with her body language. The head was nodding, I heard a few um hm, and then see finished reading and said that is me. I was flabbergasted.
Don't do that!

You have to stop nodding your head to a bunch of mess. I didn't see the person that she described about herself. She had a great personality and she was in college. She was making a change and playing for the "ooooo" – reference Look at Your Boss. – Buy it!

1 Corinthians 2:14 - The natural person does not accept the things of the Spirit of God, for they are folly to him, and he is not able to understand them because they are spiritually discerned.

It is sad but true that one's spiritual belief is often paralleled with one's personal belief. If you had spiritually discerned your situation, you would know all of the negative attributes are bloated out.

We rely so heavily on someone else's interpretation of scriptures, we don't discern scripture ourselves. We have to get to a place in which our direct relationship with God brings the appropriate scripture to memory so we can apply it to our lives.

Take a minute to answer a few questions and then discuss them with your group:

Do you believe in the Power of God?

1. _____
2. _____
3. _____

Do you feel you hear from God?

1. _____
2. _____
3. _____

What is Spiritual Discernment?

1. _____
2. _____
3. _____

Do you believe Jesus died for your sins?

1. _____
2. _____
3. _____

Do you have fond childhood memories?

1. _____

2. _____

3. _____

Is your past dictating your future? How?

1. _____

2. _____

3. _____

How often do you pray?

1. _____

2. _____

3. _____

Are you ready to be a superhero?

1. _____

2. _____

3. _____

Chapter 7

You're Not Alone

John 16:1-17:26 - ESV

"I have said all these things to you to keep you from falling away. They will put you out of the synagogues. Indeed, the hour is coming when whoever kills you will think he is offering service to God. And they will do these things because they have not known the Father, nor me. But I have said these things to you, that when their hour comes you may remember that I told them to you. "I did not say these things to you from the beginning, because I was with you. But now I am going to him who sent me, and none of you asks me, 'Where are you going?'

Prayer

My wife Jeannett has one of the most amazing life routines. It is the simplest of all routines but it pays the most dividends. She wakes up in the morning while the family is asleep takes her bible, reads it, and prays. She has been doing this for as long as I have known her. At night before she goes to bed, she gets on her knees at our bedside and prays. When someone calls with an issue, she prays. When the kids leave before school, we pray. She never forced me to do it but her habitual actions, and the connection she has with God, simply put I wanted that. She is on all accounts a prayer warrior.

The more time I spent with her the more I realized Grandma was right I was a Stiffneck.

Proverbs 31:11-12 The heart of her husband trusts in her, and he will have no lack of gain. She does him good, and not harm, all the days of her life.

I noticed she is rarely upset and when she is, she takes it to God then moves in the direction in which she is lead. She is the rock and foundation in our family; in spite of me.

Pray when you rise; pray when you lay down to sleep.

This is a short chapter because –simply put –

Prayer Changes things

Prayer gives you direction

Prayer gives you strength

My words mean nothing,

But God's Word is everything.

Take a minute to answer a few questions and then discuss them with your group:

Do you fear being alone?

1. _____

2. _____

3. _____

Are you a stiff neck?

1. _____

2. _____

3. _____

What is your personal improvement plan?

1. _____

2. _____

3. _____

Do you have a Spiritual Growth Routine?

1. _____

2. _____

3. _____

Do you trust God?

1. _____

2. _____

3. _____

How can you better understand the scriptures?

1. _____

2. _____

3. _____

How often do you pray?

1. _____

2. _____

3. _____

Are in a Bible Study?

1. _____

2. _____

3. _____

Chapter 8

It's Your Time

Proverbs 3:5 - ESV

Trust in the Lord with all your heart, and do not lean on your own understanding.

You Matter

Dr. Kim Scott a co-worker of mine has a great mantra – motto – phrase; "It's my time". When he speaks he reminds everyone to stop making excuses and make something happen. It's your time.

Do not lean on your own understanding. Do not rely on someone else's understanding about you.

Stop putting more weigh on someone else's opinion and please don't disregard your own opinion. Some years ago, I was confronted with a situation where a woman didn't believe in herself. She convinced herself she was a people pleaser – she would go out of her way to please people. Everyone she came in contact with she felt a need to please – she felt it was her job to please. She never took care of herself because she worried so much about everyone else. So naturally, whenever something needed to be done, everyone would ask her to do it. Rather than say no she worked, worked, worked. This went on for years. And then she met me... smh. In her mind, she was a people pleaser but in reality she did not believe in herself. She felt a desire please even when she knew a situation wasn't right; she couldn't take a stand.

I questioned her on why she would knowingly do what was wrong. I encouraged her to read the Bible and put her decisions to the GAP test.

She constantly felt hurt because her expectation was not a reality. Everyone would not return the effort she was putting out. But the reality was she didn't want to let anyone down so she often found herself in the middle; good, bad, and indifferent. There is a difference between servitude and slavitude (yea I made that up).

Let me encourage you to take a stand. When you're filling the GAP it needs to pass the integrity test.

1 Thessalonians 4:11-12 - *And to aspire to live quietly, and to mind your own affairs, and to work with your hands, as we instructed you, so that you walk properly before outsiders and be dependent on no one.*

Take a minute to answer a few questions and then discuss them with your group:

Do you believe it's your time?

1. _____

2. _____

3. _____

What changes do you need to make?

1. _____

2. _____

3. _____

What are the first three things you need to improve?

1. _____

2. _____

3. _____

Are you a people pleaser?

1. _____

2. _____

3. _____

Do you blame other people for your shortfalls?

1. _____

2. _____

3. _____

Take ownership for the last three negative situations that happened in your life?

1. _____

2. _____

3. _____

How often do you pray?

1. _____

2. _____

3. _____

What can you do to let go of your past?

1. _____

2. _____

3. _____

Chapter 9

Walk the Talk

Proverbs 14:23 - ESV

In all toil there is profit, but mere talk tends only to poverty.

Questions

Who am I'? When did we learn limitations? When did it become easier to believe "I can't"? What happened to the belief of "I can" and "I will?" Do you remember your teenager rebellious spirit of I dare you to try and stop me? What happened to your boldness? When did you stop believing in the plan God laid out for you? Did you ever know the plan? When did you start down this path of deception? And finally, who put your fire out? Is there something you do every day that brings you joy? Is there something you do for someone else that brings you joy? have you veered off course? Are you your worst enemy – or should I say "inner me?"

What type of verbal exchange do you have with your inner voice? Is that voice an ally or an enemy? By who, what, and when was that voice developed? Who shaped that voice? Whose voice do you hear in your mind when decisions are being made about your life? How often do you hear God's Voice; the voice from the knowledge of His Word? Have you ever done something out of fear or with a fearful spirit? When did these voices start to turn on you?

Is it in alignment and in direction of God's Word? If not, why are you giving that voice so much power over your actions? Where did the source get its power over you? how much weight do you give those thoughts? Are the thoughts negative or positive? Have you ever said this to yourself? Why are you so hard on yourself? What actions have you taking to improve upon the critiques? When you start criticizing yourself – what voice do you hear? How do you recondition your mind after years and years of battering? After years and years of believing your self-worth aint what it ought to be? What song do you play when you have stuff on your mind? When the voices are going off in your head condemning and torturing you? What songs are you listening to? Do you like the song because of the beginning and are you getting to the end? What is your theme song? What is your theme song? Is it triumphant? You ever listen to a song that makes you want to run out the door and tackle the world? What does your physical reflection present that your mental reflection is lacking? When you close your eyes and think about yourself, are you Spiderman or Batman? Who are you when you close your eyes? Now, what happens when you open them? What did you see that person accomplish that you couldn't do yourself? As a matter of fact have you ever met you?

If you met yourself for the first time, what would be your first impression? Now – stop – when you thought about yourself whose voice did you hear? Are you so beaten down that you cannot find one nice thing to say about you? Who is the person that co-signs on all your misery? Were you able to positively talk about yourself for 30 seconds? Are you being realistic? How do you like you so far? Did you see how you read over the words "enemy" and "inner me" as if it were the same word? Is it me or is there is a lot of talk today about a person's appearance? How you look on the outside? If we opened you up today, what will the content reveal? Who are you? When you were putting together that 30 second "me" speech, how much was fluff? How much were you trying to be "the you," you wanted to be? How do you treat people? Do you have the correct outward appearance? What does this mean in relationship to you "being you?" How much time do you spend chasing a dream that is not purposed? How much time do you spend searching the scriptures, praying, and discerning the moves you make based on the test? Is it good and acceptable and perfect in the eyes of God? When you look in the mirror at your adorning, can you honestly say that is who you are? What is on your mind? How then do you take what has been presented and apply it to your life? Will it take another two years for you to make the necessary changes to be comfortable in your own skin? Do you have more excuses than you have results? How do we get it done? Where is your commitment to self?

Psalm 106:25 They murmured in their tents, and did not obey the voice of the Lord.

Listen to your inner voice; God's Voice... Shhhh, listen;

BElieve in YOUrself!

Notes

Notes

Notes

Notes

Sneak 👁 Peek!!!

*** *Unedited – Rough Draft* ***

Preview of the forthcoming book:

STIFF-NECK!!!
PEOPLE –LEADERSHIP-PASTOR

© 2015, James Sutton Jr., Mount Holly, NC

ALL RIGHTS RESERVED. No part of this book may be reproduced or transmitted in any form or by any means without written permission from the author.

Stiffneck

Proverbs 29:11 NIV: A man who remains stiff-necked after many rebukes will suddenly be destroyed--without remedy.

I first researched the word Stiffneck when I graduated from Bible College and my wife's grandmother an Evangelist whom I respect and love, right before Prayer, she looked at me and stated "You're a Sniff-Neck"–and popped me on the back of the neck! It came out of the blue – I was not certain what she was talking about. So of course I questioned why she made the statement. I was unfamiliar with the term and waited on her to explain. She did her grandma pause, looked me in the eye, and she said "You don't believe in nothing! - you have too much education and you don't rely on the Holy Spirit." I must have had an Arsenio Hall moment because I am sure my facial expression read "things that make you say hmmm." Through the years you learned not to argue with grandma; you especially don't question her on the bible. That night, I prayed and I diligently searched the scriptures, as I was taught in Bible College, because I wasn't certain if I was insulted or chastised; maybe both.

Stiff Neck

Acts 7:51 Ye stiffnecked and uncircumcised in heart and ears, ye do always resist the Holy Ghost: as your fathers did, so do ye.

The Bible is clear on the definition of sniff neck – One that resists the Holy Ghost. For the life of me I could not figure out why I was called out by my grandma about being one that did not rely on the Holy Spirit –

I do not know why one would believe having an education is a cause not to believe in the greatest blessing Jesus released to defeat the enemy. I understand that the battle is not against flesh and blood. But here I am an Ox – The term stiff neck came from the fact that farmers used Oxen to plow fields in ancient Israel – The ox would stiffen its neck to prevent the farmer from going in the appropriate direction.

The Bible tells us to search the scriptures – Often time the congregation blindly listens to the Word being preached without doing their own due diligence of insuring that the Word being preached is in line with the Word written. It requires one to search the scriptures. Read the Bible! Be a part of a group reading the scriptures and searching for clarification. It is not to say that one does not believe what that pastor is saying but the Bereans were eager and examined daily what Paul spoke to insure it lined up with the Word of God.

> Acts 17:11 NLT And the people of Berea were more open-minded than those in Thessalonica, and they listened eagerly to Paul's message. They searched the Scriptures day after day to see if Paul and Silas were teaching the truth.

When we look at the parables and scriptures pertaining to Jesus ministry, the mindset of the ox plowing the land takes on deeper meaning. Jesus uses parables in relationship to the Harvest as a means to communicate to its followers.

The pulpit, the congregations, the officers must all communicate and be mindful of the seeds sown. One must be mindful that seeds are sown in deeds as well as words. With the understanding that God is not mocked the stiff neck mentality often time by nature of the ox will hold the sower accountable failing to realize this is God's place – The Bible tells us to communicate to him that teaches in all good things.

> 7 Do not be deceived and deluded and misled; God will not allow Himself to be sneered at (scorned, disdained, or mocked [a]by mere pretensions or professions, or by His precepts being set aside.) [He inevitably deludes himself who attempts to delude God.] For whatever a man sows, that and [b]that only is what he will reap.8 For he who sows to his own flesh (lower nature, sensuality) will from the flesh reap decay and ruin and destruction, but he who sows to the Spirit will from the Spirit reap eternal life.9 And let us not lose heart and grow weary and faint in acting nobly and doing right, for in due time and at the appointed season we shall reap, if we do not loosen and relax our courage and faint.

We are going to embark on a walk that will address some concerns – shed some light – and hopefully end with accountability and discernment. This work is not meant to bash though some will receive its content as direct. It is meant to be direct because we are in a time and at a place where we must hold -

Chapter 1

How is the Stiff neck mindset developed?

As a travelling military man and scholar, I've served in more churches then I can remember. I've had positions and I continue to follow my calling. And this work is a part of the calling to assist the folk that have developed the stiff-neck mindset. I've found through my many years in ministry that even well intentioned churches can perpetuate the stiff-neck mindset. It is developed by the seeds planted in the church. From religious relationships, from the pulpit, from the actions of leadership in the church – Now it is easy to say and condemn those that feel the church is the cause of any pain but self-righteous condemnation from the church is the cause of the stiff neck mentality. If one were to observe the church from the outside looking in – the actions and lack of actions by the people in the church, from the pastors of the church, and the leaders of the church – these actions will make it possible for anyone to believe and follow the stiff neck mentality- I see leadership tell people to give it to God yet they themselves live at the altar praying for the same miracle they asked God to give them every time they are in the Church – yes we are to pray without ceasing but we are not to keep

> *7Be not deceived; God is not mocked: for whatsoever a man soweth, that shall he also reap.*
>
> *8For he that soweth to his flesh shall of the flesh reap corruption; but he that soweth to the Spirit shall of the Spirit reap life everlasting.*
>
> *9And let us not be weary in well doing: for in due season we shall reap, if we faint not.*

"You reap, what you sow." – Seed falling on good ground.

Educated Christians:

For some strange reason I have found that education is not valued in religious circles; unless it is the Pastor. Often time, I hear Pastors speak to the congregation and tell them or should I say imply that nothing is required for one to be successful in life. They double-talk the idea and state God can do anything – he can make a Doctor out of anyone. Now in my stiff-necked mindset – I do not disagree that one can do anything through Jesus Christ – the scripture clearly states in Philippians 4:13 that "I can do all things through Christ who give me strength." I guess the question is whether one is required to do anything other than sit and wait. The concern I've heard and seen is we explain the power of God... we explain the purpose and power of Faith and we run over the fact that Faith is a verb. It requires action! Then we just lead folk to pray –sit and wait. So at this point I am questioning if that is a sniff-neck mentality or is it a lack of understanding coming from the pulpit to properly prepare people for advancement. We often hear from preachers stating as they are elevated the congregation will be elevated- but I have seen year after year – generation to generation the only people be elevated is the Preacher- the Stiff-neck mentality does not quite understand why one would want to be elevated without its flock when the message being preached is stay complacent and pray.

What does the Bible say about education in the traditional sense? How does it impact how one looks at education today? It is very likely that with education if not properly delivered it will cause one to question the very existence of God. However, to imply one is a Stiff-neck if one questions the unfolding of the scripture to the congregation is not being rebuked.

John 5:39 You diligently study the Scriptures because you think that by them you possess eternal life. These are the Scriptures that testify about me...

Made in the USA
Charleston, SC
02 November 2015